SHIPS

THROUGH TIME

SHIPS

THROUGH TIME

Roy Richards

RSVP

RAINTREE
STECK-VAUGHN
PUBLISHERS
The Steck-Vaughn Company

Austin, Texas

Published by Raintree Steck-Vaughn Publishers, an imprint of Steck-Vaughn Company

Macdonald Young Books
Design: Celia Hart
Illustration: Ross Watton, The Garden Studio
Commissioning Editor: Debbie Fox
Editor: Jayne Booth
Consultants: Simon Stephens and Alec Fearon C. Eng., Eur. Ing.

Raintree Steck-Vaughn Publishers staff
Editor: Kathy DeVico
Project Manager: Joyce Spicer

Photo Acknowledgments
We are grateful to the following for permission to reproduce photographs: Robert Harding (p. 16); Michael Holford (pp. 8, 12); London Science Museum (p. 28); The Master and Fellows Magdalene College, Cambridge (p. 20); National Maritime Museum (p. 24).

The Publishers would like to thank the following for their help: Kathy Baxendale; Alison Couper (Sea Containers); Bob Cripps, Gill Mace, Georgette Purches, Lisa Symes (RNLI); Eila Henderson (Lloyds Register); Hoverspeed; Keith Johnson; Emma Parkin (British Marine Industries Federation); Port of London Authority; Brian Rees (Stena Sealink Line); Dr. Margaret Rule (Mary Rose Trust); Mark Rymell; Nigel Weare (Amateur Rowing Association).

Library of Congress Cataloging-in-Publication Data

Richards, Roy.
    Ships / Roy Richards.
        p. cm. — (Through time)
    Includes index.
    ISBN 0–8172–4138–8
    1. Ships — History — Juvenile literature.
    2. Navigation — History — Juvenile literature.
    [1. Ships — History. 2. Navigation — History.]
    I. Title II. Series.
    VM150. R475   1996
    623. 8' 09 — dc20   95–23172
                                CIP
                                AC

Printed and bound in Hong Kong.
1 2 3 4 5 6 7 8 9 0 99 98 97 96 95

CONTENTS

THE FIRST BOATS

Humans have traveled by water for thousands of years. Moving on the water was easier and quicker than overland, and boats could also carry large cargoes over great distances. Through the ages, different materials have been used to make boats, depending on what was available and how good people were at building them. When people first traveled by water, they probably used a floating tree trunk. Then they learned to tie logs together or use other materials, like bundled reeds, to make rafts. Animal skins were used to make floats or to cover a framework of bamboo or willow to make a watertight boat. Some of these materials are still used today.

EGYPTIAN PAPYRUS BOAT
Papyrus reeds were a plentiful resource along the Nile River. The ancient Egyptians bundled them together to make boats.

THE KON TIKI

The *Kon Tiki* was built by explorer Thor Heyerdahl. He wanted to prove such a raft could cross the Pacific Ocean. *Kon Tiki* was a copy of an ancient South American raft and was made of long balsa wood logs. They were bound together with about 300 pieces of rope — no nails were used at all. A short, thick log across the back supported the steering oar, and two strong posts held the sail. The voyage took place in 1947 with six men on board. It lasted 95 days and was a success.

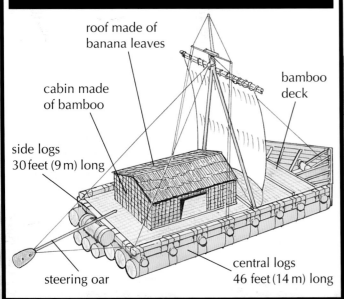

roof made of banana leaves

cabin made of bamboo

bamboo deck

side logs 30 feet (9 m) long

steering oar

central logs 46 feet (14 m) long

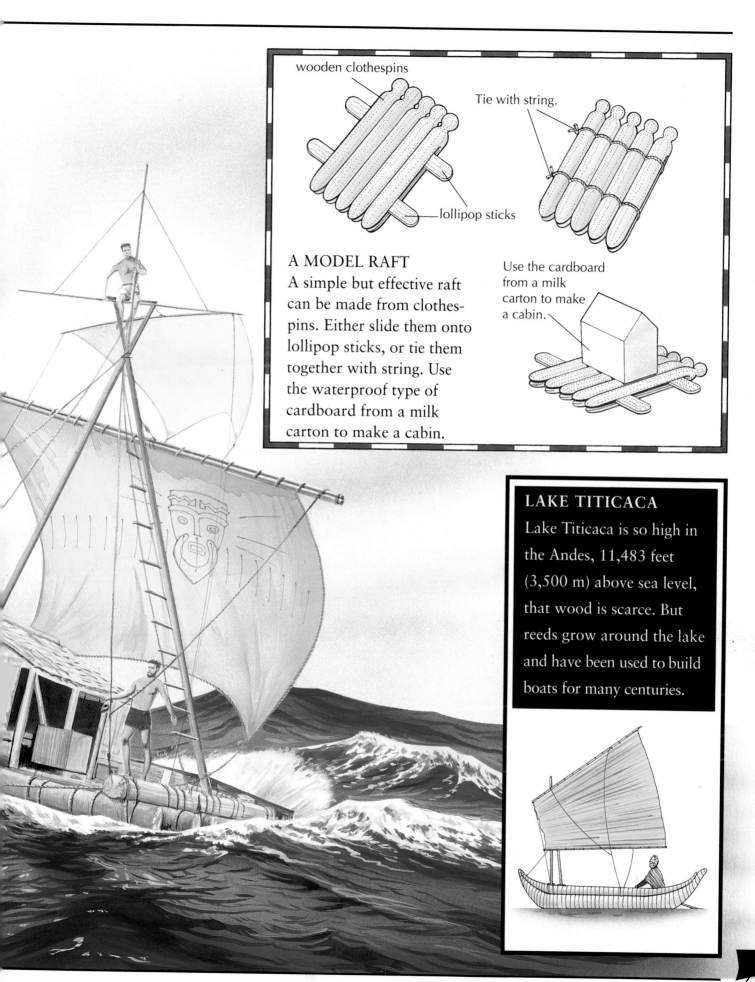

wooden clothespins

Tie with string.

lollipop sticks

A MODEL RAFT

A simple but effective raft can be made from clothespins. Either slide them onto lollipop sticks, or tie them together with string. Use the waterproof type of cardboard from a milk carton to make a cabin.

Use the cardboard from a milk carton to make a cabin.

LAKE TITICACA

Lake Titicaca is so high in the Andes, 11,483 feet (3,500 m) above sea level, that wood is scarce. But reeds grow around the lake and have been used to build boats for many centuries.

SKIN BOATS

Animal skins are a good natural material for making boats because they are light and strong, and they can be sewn together and made waterproof. They were used as floats or to cover a frame to make a hull — a hollowed-out boat. Learning to make a hull was an important advance in technology because boats could be built to different sizes, and they were more seaworthy (see page 22).

(see page 22)

Genghis Khan, the Mongol conqueror, used goat skins blown up like balloons as floats. This way his army crossed the great Oxus River, in Central Asia.

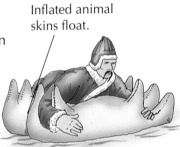

Inflated animal skins float.

The prehistoric coracle is still used today on rivers in Wales and south-west England. The coracler paddles with the stream to move sideways across the river.

One-person coracles are light enough to carry.

North American Inuit use kayaks for hunting because they move very quickly. Kayaks are made of light driftwood frames, with sealskins sewn together and stretched over them.

Some Inuit now use painted canvas to cover kayaks.

STAYING DRY

The Inuit people developed the kayak — a type of canoe with a covered top. The top helped to prevent the boat from being flooded in rough waters and kept the paddler dry. The Inuit wore animal skins to keep them warm and dry and even laced their clothes into the skin covering the kayak to keep the boat watertight. Today, paddlers wear wet suits and spray/splash decks — a sort of apron that seals the top of the kayak.

safety helmet

spray/splash deck

life jacket

wet suit

PADDLING

Paddling is a way of moving and steering a boat through the water using body strength. The first paddles were probably just branches, but today the most modern kayak paddles are made of Kevlar® carbon fiber — the same material used to build Formula One racing cars. The paddler puts the blade of the paddle in front and pulls the boat through the water.

Single paddles are used in open-top canoes. Twisting the paddle in the water or pulling harder on one side also steers the canoe.

Double paddles are used in kayaks. The blades are set at an angle to each other, so there is less air resistance on the blade out of the water.

DUGOUT CANOES

Another way to make a boat hull is to hollow out a tree trunk. Thousands of years ago, people from Polynesia used dugout canoes to explore and settle new islands all over the Pacific. They traveled many thousands of miles. Canoes like these are still used in the South Seas, the Amazon, and Africa.

OUTRIGGERS

Tree trunks were chipped out with an ax and shaped on the outside to make them cut through the water. Trees near the water's edge were best, because they could be launched more easily. But boats like these could easily roll over and tip the canoeist into the water. Then people discovered that adding another log as a float would stabilize the dugout. The log is placed parallel to the canoe and attached to it by long poles. This log float is called an outrigger.

ADDING A SAIL

A sail can be added to an outrigger canoe. The float is kept windward, which is the side the wind is blowing from. It acts as a counterbalance to the push of the wind on the sail.

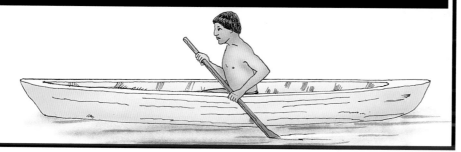

outrigger

poles to attach the outrigger to the dugout

dugout canoe

hole for a mast

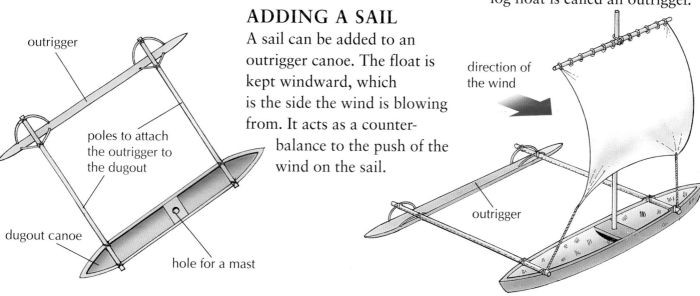

direction of the wind

outrigger

A MODEL OUTRIGGER

You can build an outrigger using a cigar or tablet tube or balsa wood, and pencils or dowels. Tie the parts together as shown with thread or thin string. Vary the distance between the "outrigger" and the "dugout" and notice the effect on your boat's stability.

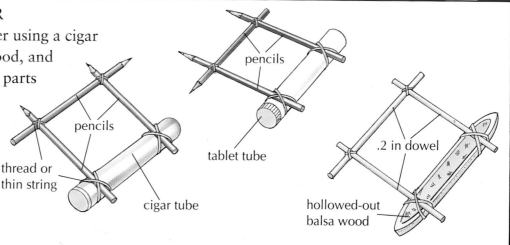

pencils

pencils

tablet tube

thread or thin string

cigar tube

.2 in dowel

hollowed-out balsa wood

ANCIENT GALLEYS

The Roman galleys above are a carving on Trajan's Column, which was built in A.D. 114 to record Rome's victory over the Dacians in A.D. 101–106. Here you can see the Roman rowers using oar power.

Paddling was probably the first method people used to propel their boats. The next advance was rowing. People discovered that by facing the back of the boat and pulling a long oar through the water, they were using their body strength more efficiently. The oar had to be pivoted on the side of the boat. This way longer oars could be used, and bigger boats could be propelled. But rowing created a new problem — how to steer the boat. And so steering oars and then rudders were developed as ways of directing ships. The ancient Greeks and Romans built large fighting ships with many rowers on board, as the illustration of this Roman war galley shows.

THE GREEK TRIREME

Greek triremes also had a large pointed battering ram at the front for sinking ships. They could move very rapidly — up to 8 knots — and their speed gave great force to the ram.

In a bireme, there were two tiers of oars — about 120 men.

Biremes were about 79 feet (24 m) long and 9.8 feet (3 m) wide.

In a trireme, there were three tiers of oars — about 170 men.

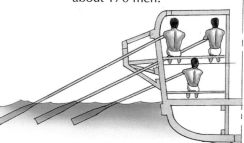

Triremes were about 141 feet (43 m) long and 16 feet (5 m) wide.

PUSHING WITH OARS

Fill a dishpan with water. Use a wooden spoon as an oar. With the bowl of the spoon just below the surface of the water, push your "oar" through the water from back to front.

Try it with a short oar and then with a long oar. Now paddle with your spoon by moving it from front to back. Which is the easier way to move the water?

short oar

long oar

A ROMAN MERCHANT SHIP

The Romans had a huge empire. They brought goods over great distances to supply Rome, and they traded with many other nations. To carry their cargoes, they developed merchant ships. They could set the sails to steer the ship as well as to move it. Two large oars at the stern were used to improve the steering.

RUDDERS

The rudder was invented by the Chinese over 5,000 years ago, and it is still used today. It is a flat piece of wood or metal hinged to the back of a vessel, and it stands upright in the water. The rudder works by pushing against the flow of water passing along the hull, which causes the ship to change direction. This is one of the easiest ways to steer a moving ship. Rudders have great force because they are deep in the water and have more surface area than steering oars, so they are strong enough to steer large ships, too.

Large rowing boats have rudders to help when steering. Some have ropes attached to them. By pulling the ropes, the person sitting at the back of the boat can steer.

steering ropes

rudder

THE DEVELOPMENT OF STEERING

Early travel by water was probably in small boats that floated with the currents in the water. As boats became larger and people wanted to travel against the wind or currents, they had to invent ways of steering. Although the rudder was invented 5,000 years ago, it wasn't used in the West until the twelfth century.

Early boats could be pushed along and steered, using a long pole. People still do this today — it is called punting.

You can steer using a paddle by pulling harder on one side of the boat.

Over 4,500 years ago, the Egyptians were among the first to steer their boats by using two large steering oars at the stern.

TILLERS

Another device for moving a rudder is a tiller. This is a horizontal bar attached to the top of the rudder. The tiller is kept parallel with the boat to make it travel straight ahead. Turning the tiller to the right moves the rudder to the left.

This causes the water to push against it and turns the boat to the left.

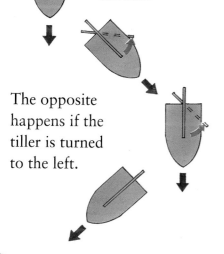

The opposite happens if the tiller is turned to the left.

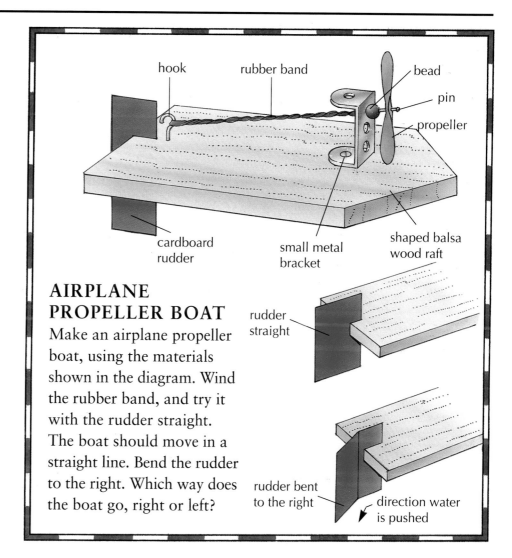

hook rubber band bead pin propeller

cardboard rudder small metal bracket shaped balsa wood raft

AIRPLANE PROPELLER BOAT

Make an airplane propeller boat, using the materials shown in the diagram. Wind the rubber band, and try it with the rudder straight. The boat should move in a straight line. Bend the rudder to the right. Which way does the boat go, right or left?

rudder straight

rudder bent to the right direction water is pushed

The Chinese invented rudders. They controlled the rudder with a tiller.

As ships became larger, mechanical help was needed to move the tiller and rudder.

Until the early eighteenth century, the whipstaff was used to move the tiller. It was difficult to control in rough waters.

Then the wheel was developed in the early eighteenth century. Turning the wheel pulled ropes attached to the tiller, which then controlled the rudder. This is an easier way to control the tiller than the whipstaff.

whipstaff

tiller

rudders

wheel

ropes and pulleys

tiller

THE VIKING SHIP

Figureheads were often carved on the bow in the shape of snakes or dragons.

The Vikings from Scandinavia are famed for their seamanship. Their ships were strong and well designed to withstand rough oceans as well as traveling up rivers. The shape of the bow of the ships helped them to cut through the water, while the flatter bottom gave them stability. The ships could be rowed, but the Vikings also used large, square sails that were mounted on strong oak masts. Between A.D. 800 and 1070, the Vikings dominated the seas of northern Europe, reaching the Mediterranean, and even crossing the Atlantic Ocean to Iceland, Greenland, and North America.

A SHALLOW DRAFT

The Viking ships were built out of planks using the "clinker" method. This means each plank overlapped the one beneath it. Any gaps between the planks were filled, or caulked, with animal hair soaked in tar. Using these methods, the Vikings could make a hull of any size watertight. Warships were narrow and shallow so that they could make their way up rivers and estuaries easily and be beached safely. Merchant ships for carrying cargoes were also shallow but broader.

yard

T-shaped upright

STOWING THE SAIL

When rowing ashore, the sail and the yard were laid along T-shaped uprights. This gave more deck space, and the ship was easier to control and more stable because the sail's weight was over the centerline.

Make a hull out of balsa wood.

MAKE A SAILING SHIP

You can make your own Viking ship. Carefully cut out the hull from balsa wood. You can use a bamboo skewer for the mast. Cut out a square sail from paper, and attach it to the mast. Now launch your ship in a bowl of water. Blow at it from different directions to see how the sail catches the wind.

Punch through a paper sail with a bamboo skewer.

Attach the sail and mast to the hull.

LACK OF WIND

We know that the Vikings had different types of ships — some for trade and others for war. The ships' sails were made out of panels of homespun wool that were sewn together. If there was no wind, or if a battle was to be fought, the Vikings could row their ships. They put their oars through wooden ports and sometimes lowered the mast and sail. There were no fixed rowing benches, and each sailor probably sat on his sea chest.

SAILING BEFORE THE WIND

It was easier to sail a Viking ship when the wind was behind it. If the wind was too far around to the side, it would have rolled the ship over. This was because Viking ships didn't have a deep keel (see opposite).

The Vikings probably used ropes to hold the sail to catch the wind, although we have no archaeological evidence for this.

DEVELOPMENT OF THE SAIL

Many types of sails have been used through the ages. Here are some different sail arrangements. Sailing ships have to adjust the size of the sails to suit the strength of the wind. If the wind is very strong, the sail size must be reduced. This is called reefing.

2500 B.C.
The Egyptian trader had a square sail. In storms, the size of the sail had to be reduced by lowering the yard. This was an early method of reefing.

MIDDLE AGES TO TODAY
Chinese junk sails were made in sections, so they could be rolled up and down, according to the wind's strength.

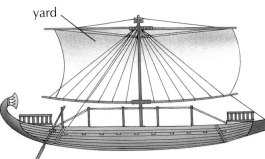

yard

bamboo supports

SAILING CLOSE TO THE WIND

No sailing ship can sail directly into the wind, but some can sail "closer" or more toward it than others. Modern yachts with a deep keel can set their sails so that they move forward at a sharp angle toward the wind. This is called beating. They can also go forward with the wind blowing across their sides. This is called reaching.

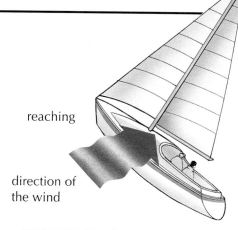

reaching

direction of the wind

direction of the wind

beating

STEERING A COURSE

To travel in the direction of the wind, sailing ships have to follow a zig-zag course, by beating one way into the wind and then turning and beating the other way. This method is called tacking.

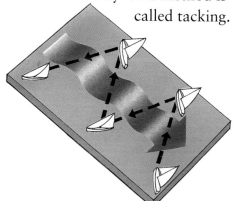

ADDING A KEEL

A keel helps to prevent a sailing ship from being pushed over on its side by the force of the wind on the sails. Make a keel for your Viking ship, by attaching a nail to the bottom. Does it make your ship more stable?

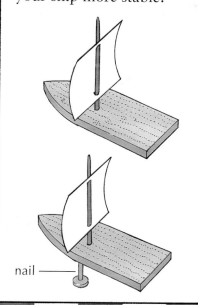

nail

NINETEENTH CENTURY

This square-rigged ship could adjust the size of its sails and the angle at which they were set to get the best use of the wind.

TODAY

On a modern yacht, the front edge of the main sail is attached to the mast, making it rigid. This means it can sail "closer" into the direction of the wind.

main sail

keel

THE FIRST WARSHIP

The Tudor Kings, Henry VII and Henry VIII, designed the first warships, which led to England's dominance at sea during the sixteenth century. These ships had strong hulls and decks that could take the weight of heavy guns. But heavy guns had to be put in lower decks to maintain the ship's stability. This meant holes, called ports, had to be cut low in the hull for the guns to point through, but they also had to be able to shut so the ship could stay watertight. The need for gun ports led to a new way of building hulls. Instead of clinker planking (see page 16), where the planks overlap each other, the Tudors

THE MARY ROSE
The *Mary Rose* was built in 1510 and reconstructed in 1534. It sank in 1545 and was not found until 1967. It was finally raised to the surface in 1982.

used carvel planking, where they were attached, edge to edge. In July 1545, the *Mary Rose* was ready for battle against the French in Portsmouth Harbor. The ship was very heavy. As it turned, it tilted over, and because its hull was low in the water and its gun ports were open, the water rushed in. This made it tilt even more, until it capsized and quickly sank.

ARMAMENTS

Until the sixteenth century, sea battles were won by boarding the enemy's ships. With guns, a navy could sink enemy ships from a distance. The *Mary Rose* had 91 guns made of bronze or iron. When it was rebuilt in 1534, heavier guns were attached, adding to its weight. Of the crew of 700 men, 285 were heavily armed soldiers.

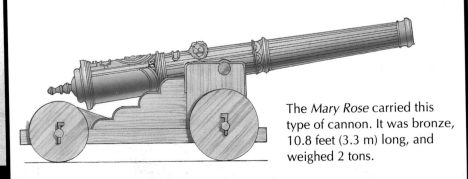

The *Mary Rose* carried this type of cannon. It was bronze, 10.8 feet (3.3 m) long, and weighed 2 tons.

SEAWORTHINESS

To be seaworthy, a ship has to be stable enough to stay right side up even when it has to turn or in rough waters, and it has to stay afloat. A ship will only stay afloat if it is lighter than the weight of water it displaces, or pushes aside. In the nineteenth century, some ship owners overloaded their ships on purpose so they would sink and the owner could collect the insurance money. They were known as "coffin ships," because many sailors drowned. As a result, Plimsoll marks were introduced as part of the Merchant Shipping Act of 1876 to prevent overloading. Plimsoll marks are named after Samuel Plimsoll, an English politician, who worked hard to introduce the new law.

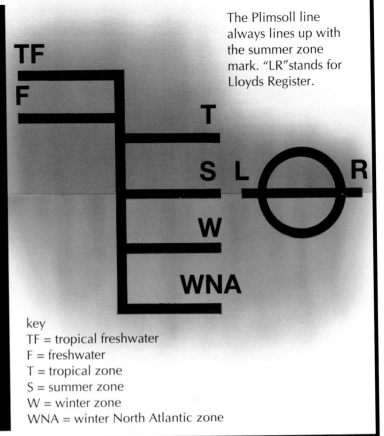

The Plimsoll line always lines up with the summer zone mark. "LR" stands for Lloyds Register.

key
TF = tropical freshwater
F = freshwater
T = tropical zone
S = summer zone
W = winter zone
WNA = winter North Atlantic zone

LOADING SHIPS ON DIFFERENT WATERS

Great care must be taken when loading ships. Heavy cargoes should be put at the bottom and distributed evenly over the front, back, and along the sides of the ship. This keeps the ship from tilting or even toppling over in the water. Plimsoll marks measure how much cargo a ship can safely carry in different water conditions. To set loading levels, the world is divided into zones. The tropical zone has better weather conditions than the winter North Atlantic zone, so ships are allowed to load deeper. As freshwater contains no salt, it is lighter than seawater, so ships lie deeper in freshwater.

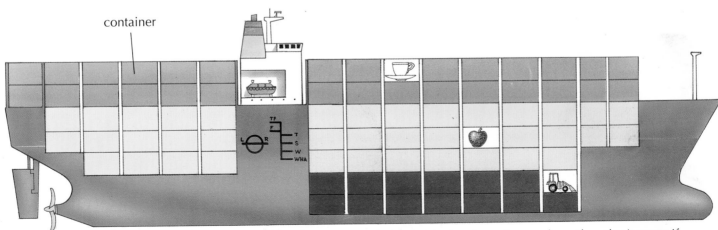

Containers carry all sorts of cargoes, such as china, fruit, and machinery. Containers can be loaded on and off trucks at the port.

Cargoes must be stowed securely so they don't move if the ship rolls. If they shift to one side, they could keep the ship from righting itself.

THE MARBLE GAME

Cut some equal-sized pieces of modeling clay, but don't cut them too big.

Give each of your friends a piece to mold into a saucer-shaped boat. Float the boats in water. Which one holds the most marbles before it sinks?

You could then let each of your friends make his or her own shaped boat. (Again, make sure that you give each of them the same amount of modeling clay.)

Now test the boats for stability.

Make each of your boats as before, but this time put a wooden building block in it. Then add another block and then another, until the tower of blocks is so unstable that the boat topples to one side. Who has made the most stable boat? Is it the same as the one that held the greatest load?

SELF-RIGHTING BOATS

A lifeboat is specially designed to cope with terrible weather conditions. The pilothouse is watertight, which means that air is trapped at the top of the boat. If the boat rolls on its side or turns upside-down, the light top and the heavy engines at the bottom pull the boat the right way up again. There are also airtight compartments in the hull, so if the boat is punctured below the waterline it will still stay afloat. These compartments also give the lifeboat buoyancy and stability.

engine

pilothouse

pilothouse

airtight compartment

airtight compartment

engine

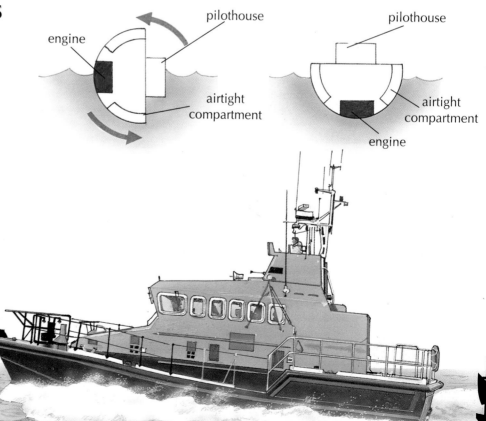

NAVIGATION

CAPTAIN COOK 1728–1779
Captain Cook made three voyages of exploration. On the first, he charted New Zealand. On the second, he reached the farthest point south recorded until then, and on the third he reached the farthest point north.

In huge oceans, there are no landmarks to help guide ships. Navigation is the way ships at sea know their position and decide the direction they need to take to reach their destination. Modern ships have very advanced technology to help them find their way, but early navigators had lots of problems to overcome. To know exactly where they were going, they had to know the direction they were taking, their latitude, and their longitude. Once people had learned how to find these things out and record them, they could chart new lands accurately and plan the safest routes for their sea journeys. Closer to land, lighthouses help a crew to locate a ship's position. Below, the great navigator, Captain Cook, is using a sextant to calculate his latitude.

CHARTING

Captain Cook was very skilled at making maps of the new lands he explored. On his first voyage, he spent six months accurately charting New Zealand. He didn't have a chronometer and had to observe the moon and use complex mathematical tables to figure out his position along the coastline (see page 26).

Captain Cook's first voyage of exploration

HARRISON'S CHRONOMETER

In 1759 John Harrison won a competition to solve the problem of measuring longitude. He invented an accurate chronometer, or sea clock, which only lost 2.7 seconds a day. With an accurate timekeeper, navigators could calculate how far they had traveled east or west (see page 26). Captain Cook took a copy of the Harrison chronometer on his second and third voyages.

copies of the Harrison chronometer made by Larcum Kendall for Captain Cook

LATITUDE AND LONGITUDE

To find out where they were, people invented imaginary lines, called longitude and latitude, to divide up the Earth. If you know your longitude and latitude, you can pinpoint your position anywhere on Earth. Lines of longitude tell you how far east or west you are of the Prime Meridian — the line of longitude that runs through Greenwich in London. Lines of latitude tell you how many degrees north or south of the Equator you are. Centuries ago, people learned how to find their latitude, how far north or south they were, by observing the position of the sun or a star in the sky in relation to the horizon. But longitude remained a problem until the eighteenth century.

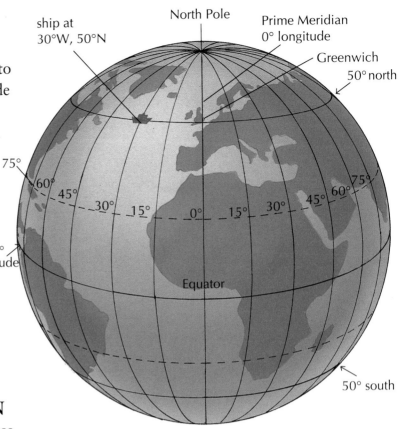

TIME ZONES AND NAVIGATION

Harrison's chronometer was important, because it enabled navigators to calculate their longitude accurately for the first time. They did this by comparing the time in Greenwich from their chronometer with noon wherever they were. The Earth is a sphere, and so it spins 360 degrees every 24 hours. In an hour, the Earth moves through 360 ÷ 24 = 15 degrees. So, if it is 2 P.M. in Greenwich and noon where the ship is, the ship must have traveled westward by 2 × 15 = 30 degrees.

THE DEVELOPMENT OF NAVIGATION

The most important developments in navigation have overcome three basic problems — working out direction, calculating latitude, and calculating longitude. In about 1000 B.C., the Chinese discovered that lodestone points to the north, which eventually led to the invention of the compass. Since then, people have invented and improved methods of finding their way.

By attaching a piece of lodestone to a piece of straw and floating the straw in a bowl of water, people made a simple compass. Mediterranean people did this in the twelfth century.

Better compasses were developed later that showed all four directions. A magnetized needle was balanced on a spindle, so it could rotate until it rested in a north/south direction. But magnetic compasses only point to magnetic north, which is slightly different than true north (see glossary). Modern gyroscopic compasses always point to true north.

MAKE A MAGNETIC COMPASS

To make a magnetic compass, hold a needle firmly, and stroke it from one end to the other with a magnet. Do this about 30 times. Always stroke in one direction. This magnetizes the needle. Tape the needle to a thin slice of cork. Place this in a dish of water. It will come to rest pointing north/ south. Cut a circle of cardboard. Then cut out the middle to make a ring. Mark the ring with the points of the compass. Place it on top of the dish. Rotate the ring of cardboard until the compass needle lines up with "N" for north. Your compass now shows north, south, east, and west.

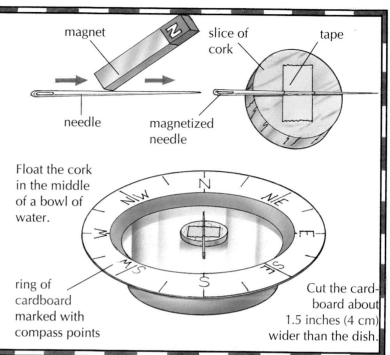

magnet · slice of cork · tape

needle · magnetized needle

Float the cork in the middle of a bowl of water.

ring of cardboard marked with compass points

Cut the cardboard about 1.5 inches (4 cm) wider than the dish.

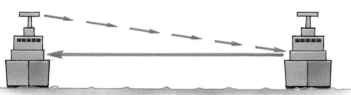

radar pulse transmitted

If there is another ship, the radar pulse is reflected back.

Radar pulses travel at the speed of light. It takes a few seconds for radar pulses to be transmitted around 360 degrees. Radar calculates the other ship's position, direction, and speed from the echo it receives.

AVOIDING OTHER SHIPS

Today, there are many ships sailing along the world's busy sea routes. It is important not to bump into other vessels. This is prevented by using radar. The radar transmits pulses of energy, one after another, around 360 degrees. If an echo returns from another ship, the radar calculates its position, direction, and speed by measuring how long the echo takes to return. Ships can detect land using radar, too.

CALCULATING LATITUDE

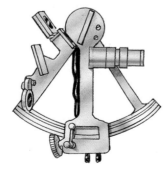

A cross staff was an early and inaccurate way of measuring the position of the sun or stars in relation to the horizon to calculate latitude.

The sextant was invented by Johann Mayer, in 1757. This device can measure the precise angle of the sun or a star to the Earth.

CALCULATING LONGITUDE

Longitude was calculated using more and more accurate clocks, until better devices were invented in this century. Radio signals from land stations and satellites can now be read by special computers to give the precise position of ships. They do this by comparing the time it takes for each signal to reach the ship.

POWERED SHIPS

THE CHARLOTTE DUNDAS
The first ship powered by steam was the *Charlotte Dundas*, built in 1801. It had a single paddle wheel at the stern.

For thousands of years, people depended on the wind or their own muscle power to move their ships. Then, at the beginning of the nineteenth century, steam engines were adapted so that they could propel ships. As people's skills in making engines developed, so did their other technical skills, like inventing new ways to propel ships and building ships of iron instead of wood. With new sources of power and new materials, larger and larger ships could be built. Today we have supertankers that are up to 1,476 feet (450 m) long! Below is the *Great Eastern*, a steamship designed by Isambard Kingdom Brunel. It was propelled by paddle wheels and a propeller. It also used sails to save fuel.

PADDLES OR PROPELLERS?

The first steam engines turned a paddle wheel at the stern of the ship, or two paddle wheels at each side. But paddle wheels are not very efficient, because most of the wheel is out of the water, doing no work at all. Screw propellers, invented in the 1840s, are better because all the blades are working in the water at the same time.

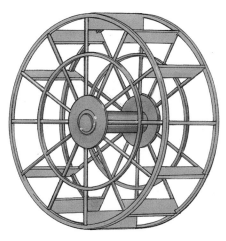

paddle wheel

In 1845 two steam-powered boats, one with paddle wheels and the other with a propeller, had a tug-of-war competition. The propeller-driven boat won!

type of propeller
used until 1860s

SIMPLE AND ADVANCED ENGINES

The first steam engines powered pistons attached to a crankshaft, which then turned the paddle wheels or a propeller. The steam was produced by burning coal in a furnace, which heated up water in a boiler. A turbine engine is more advanced than a piston engine because it uses steam or gas to turn windmill-like structures that drive the propeller directly through a gearbox. The blades of the turbine are set at an angle so that they move around when the steam or gas hits them. These engines produce a great deal of power and are very reliable.

Simple steam engine

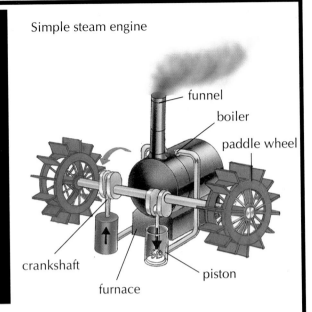

funnel
boiler
paddle wheel
crankshaft
furnace
piston

A gearbox is needed between the turbine and propeller. This is because the turbine blades turn the shaft thousands of times per minute. But the propeller can't turn as quickly, so the gearbox converts the high speed of the turbine into hundreds of turns per minute.

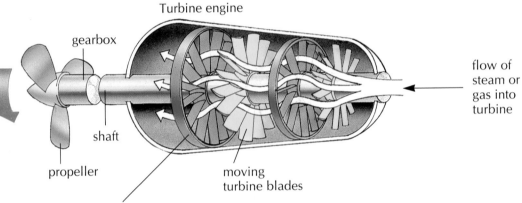

Turbine engine

gearbox
shaft
propeller

flow of steam or gas into turbine

moving turbine blades

Stationary turbine blades redirect the steam or gas onto the next set of moving blades.

THE DEVELOPMENT OF POWER

Since 1800, powered ships have developed quickly. Bigger, better engines have been invented to produce power more efficiently and move larger, faster ships.

EARLY STEAMSHIPS 1817
The first steamship to cross the English Channel was the *Elise* in 1817.

STEAM TURBINE 1884
The invention of turbine engines was a great advance, because they can drive ships much faster than piston engines. At first, coal and then oil were burned to produce the steam. Steam turbines were used in great ocean liners, like the *Mauretania* and *Lusitania*.

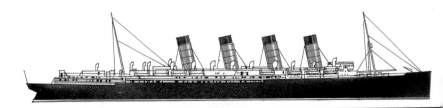

PISTON ENGINES

In these engines, pistons are moved up and down by steam, or by burning gasoline or diesel. The pistons turn a crankshaft, which, in turn, rotates a paddle wheel or propeller. Diesel engines are now the most common type of engine for ships. Each piston sits inside a cylinder. The more cylinders the ship has, the more power the engine can produce.

1. As the piston moves down in the cylinder, air is sucked in through the inlet valve.

2. The inlet valve closes. The piston moves up, which squeezes the air in the cylinder, making it very hot.

3. Diesel oil is squirted into the cylinder by an injector. The fuel catches fire, and in the hot air, it explodes and pushes the piston downward.

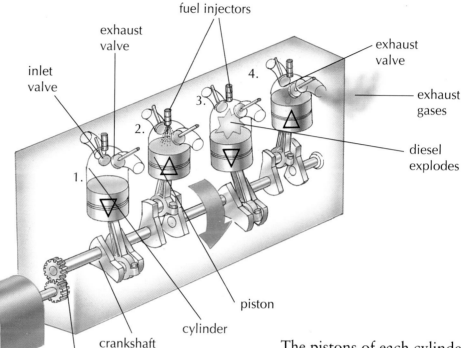

fuel injectors

exhaust valve

inlet valve

exhaust valve

exhaust gases

diesel explodes

piston

cylinder

crankshaft

gears

propeller

4. The exhaust valve opens, releasing waste gases.

The pistons of each cylinder move up and down in this process. This up and down movement turns a crankshaft, which turns the propeller.

DIESEL ENGINE 1897
Diesel engines are still common today in ships like ferries, because they can produce a lot of power cheaply. Diesel engines are also used to generate electricity for ships, like submarines and some modern warships.

GAS TURBINE SHIPS
1970s – TODAY
These ships burn fuels that produce hot expanding gases, which then turn a turbine. They can travel at high speed but use a lot of fuel. Some warships and hydrofoils use this kind of engine — so do jet aircraft!

NUCLEAR POWER
1955 – TODAY
Nuclear power is mostly used in submarines and aircraft carriers. The nuclear reactor is used to produce steam, which then turns a turbine. Nuclear power is very expensive, but it enables a ship to travel a long way without refueling.

SUBMARINES

The first underwater vessel was built in 1620, but it wasn't until the beginning of the twentieth century, when motors were invented, that submarines really started to develop. The main reason why they needed to be developed was war. Because submarines cannot be seen from the surface, they can attack unsuspecting ships with torpedoes. The German *U-boats* of World Wars I and II destroyed many enemy ships, which in turn encouraged other countries to design their own submarines. Submarines also developed so that people could explore the seabed for natural resources, like oil, or for shipwrecks, like the *Titanic*. Submarines have to be watertight and have very strong hulls that are able to withstand great pressure. The deeper a submarine goes, the greater the weight of water is above it and the greater the pressure upon it.

UP PERISCOPE
A periscope is a metal tube up to 30 feet (9 m) long. Inside are mirrors that allow the submarine's crew to see the surface of the ocean while staying hidden underwater.

SONAR
Sonar are the submarine's main sensors. There are many types. Some can detect ships hundreds of miles away by sensing the noises made by their machinery. Other sonar transmit pulses of sound and listen for echoes reflected from other submarines.

TORPEDOES
Torpedoes are guided to their target by signals sent along thin wires that link the torpedo to the submarine.

EXHAUST MAST
At periscope depth underwater, the submarine can recharge its batteries using its diesel engines. The exhaust fumes flow out through one pipe, and fresh air is drawn in through another.

CONTROL ROOM
The control room contains computers to help the crew find, track, and attack ships and other submarines. There are also controls to maneuver the submarine.

PERISCOPES

RADAR MAST

FRONT HYDROPLANE

ACCOMMODATION
Sailors sleep on bunks. They have very small lockers for clothes and other belongings.

BATTERIES
The batteries are found low down in the submarine. They power the electric motor.

AUXILIARY MACHINE ROOM
Special machinery here makes drinking water by removing salt from the seawater.

DIVING AND RISING

To make a submarine dive, valves (like large taps) in the outer hull are opened to let the air out and the seawater into the ballast tanks. The submarine becomes heavier, and it begins to sink (1). The crew controls the amount of water in the tanks until the submarine neither sinks nor rises underwater. Its depth is then controlled by the hydroplanes. To surface, compressed air is blown into the ballast tanks, which forces the water out through the valves (2). As the ballast tanks fill with air, the submarine becomes lighter and begins to rise (3).

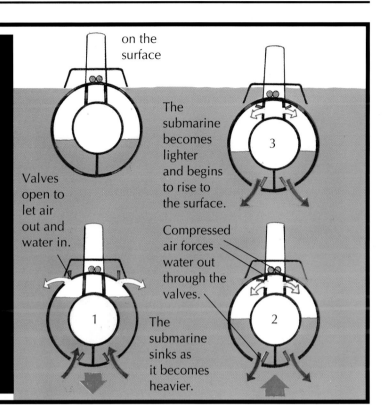

on the surface

Valves open to let air out and water in.

The submarine becomes lighter and begins to rise to the surface.

Compressed air forces water out through the valves.

The submarine sinks as it becomes heavier.

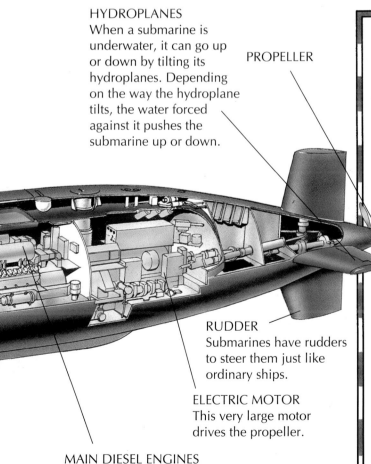

HYDROPLANES
When a submarine is underwater, it can go up or down by tilting its hydroplanes. Depending on the way the hydroplane tilts, the water forced against it pushes the submarine up or down.

PROPELLER

RUDDER
Submarines have rudders to steer them just like ordinary ships.

ELECTRIC MOTOR
This very large motor drives the propeller.

MAIN DIESEL ENGINES
These are used to charge the batteries.

A CARTESIAN DIVER

Suck some water into a medicine dropper, until it just floats in a glass of water. Put the dropper into a plastic bottle full of water. Screw on the top. Now squeeze the sides of the bottle — the dropper should sink. What happens to the water level inside the dropper? Stop squeezing the bottle, and the dropper should rise again. Squeezing the bottle increases the pressure on the water inside, which is then forced into the dropper, making it heavier, so it sinks. Releasing the bottle reduces the pressure, so the extra water inside of the dropper is sucked out, and it floats again.

water level

glass of water

Screw the top on tightly.

water level

Water level rises when the bottle is squeezed.

THE MIR SUBMERSIBLE

Submersibles are small submarines used to explore the ocean. Some have specially designed hulls that can withstand massive pressure. In 1991, two submersibles were used to film the wreck of the *Titanic*, the luxury liner that sank on its maiden voyage in 1912. It took the Mirs three hours to make the 2.5 mile (4 km) trip to the seabed where the *Titanic* lies.

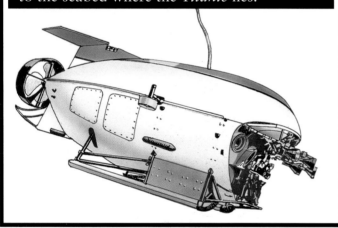

DIVING SUITS

This extraordinary diving suit has been specially designed for working in deep water. The deeper you go, the greater the pressure of the water. Normal diving suits cannot protect the diver from being crushed. This suit can withstand great pressure but also has special joints so that the person inside can move easily. Vital work, such as repairing oil rigs or underwater pipelines, can then be carried out.

The first submarine used in war was the *Turtle*, built by David Bushnell in 1776. It was made of wood, so it could not withstand the pressure of very deep water. It carried tanks that filled with water to make it sink just under the surface.

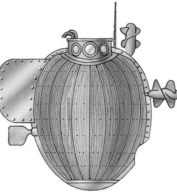

1776 (Revolutionary War)

In the mid-nineteenth century, hand and then steam power were used in *David* submarines. The *David* was the first submarine to sink an enemy ship in the Civil War, but the explosion also sank the submarine!

1861–1865 (Civil War)

THE DEVELOPMENT OF THE SUBMARINE

Early submarines, like the *Turtle*, had no engines and were driven by muscle power, but true submarines were not possible, until electric motors powered by batteries were invented. At first, gasoline and diesel engines generated electricity to charge the batteries. After World War II, nuclear power was developed to drive submarines, and nuclear missiles were introduced as a new kind of weapon.

A WORKING MODEL SUBMARINE

You can make a working model of a craft that will sink and then rise like a submarine from a plastic bottle. You can operate it with some plastic tubing or a rubber hose that is 5 feet (1.5 m) long. First, cut two holes in the bottle toward the base.

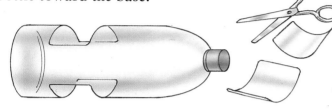

Load the bottle with pebbles or marbles, and put it into a bucket of water so that it is upright on its base. Make sure that the top is screwed on tightly.

Now insert your tubing through one of the holes, and blow into it.

The bottle should rise, because the air you are blowing into the bottle will force the water out of the bottle and make it light enough to float. If the bottle is too heavy, remove some of the pebbles or marbles.

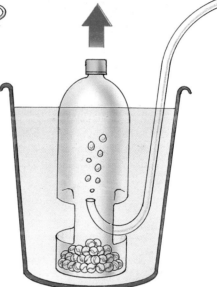

To make your submarine sink again, simply unscrew the bottle top to let the air escape.

By 1900, gasoline engines were used to power American *Holland* submarines.

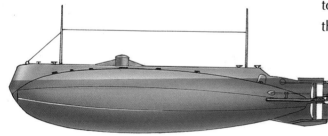

1890s – 1900

Diesel engines are used today in some submarines. But diesel engines create exhaust fumes, so the submarine has to rise almost to the surface, so it can release the fumes through a pipe and take in fresh air.

1897 – TODAY

In nuclear submarines, reactors make steam that drives turbines. These submarines could stay underwater for several years, but the crew has to surface for fresh air and food supplies. Underwater, the crew breathes air that is purified by special equipment.

1955 – TODAY

HYDROFOIL AND HOVERCRAFT

THE FIRST HYDROFOIL
The first hydrofoil to be tested successfully was built by Enrico Forlanini in Italy, in 1906. The propellers for this hydrofoil were in the air instead of underwater.

Most ships have to force their way through the water to move forward, which limits their speed. The deeper the ship's hull sits in the water, the more water it has to push out of the way when it is moving. But hydrofoils and hovercraft are specially designed to ride above the water, which makes them faster than ordinary ships. A hydrofoil has "wings" built underneath that lift the hull up out of the water when it reaches a certain speed. A hydrofoil is known as a "semisubmersible" ship, because only the foils are in the water when it is at cruising speed. Hovercraft are not really ships at all, because they don't even touch the water! They "fly" on a cushion of air just above the surface. They can travel overland, too.

THE HYDROFOIL
Because the hull of a hydrofoil lifts out of the water, there is less friction between the ship and the water. So it can travel at speeds of up to 55 knots. In rough waters, the foils just cut straight through the waves, and flaps on the foils can be adjusted to keep the ship stable. As the hydrofoil slows down, the hull sinks back into the water like a normal ship.

two different designs of hydrofoil

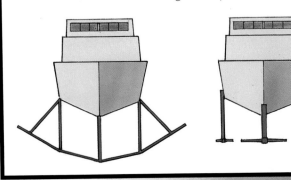

HYDRODYNAMICS

The shape of the foil lifts the boat out of the water. As the boat picks up speed, water is forced over the curved surface of the foil faster than along the flat surface. So there is more pressure beneath that pushes the foil upward.

The flow of water is faster over the top of the foil.

direction of travel

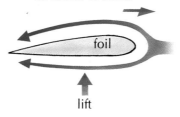

foil

lift

More pressure underneath the foil causes lift.

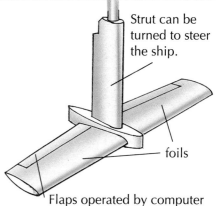

Strut can be turned to steer the ship.

foils

Flaps operated by computer help raise the ship out of the water and keep it stable.

UP IT GOES

You can simulate how the wings on a hydrofoil work.

Fold a sheet of paper in half.

Curve and glue the top half to the bottom half.

Punch a hole through both sheets. Push a piece of drinking straw through the holes.

Thread a piece of string through the straw. Ask a friend to blow on the wing.

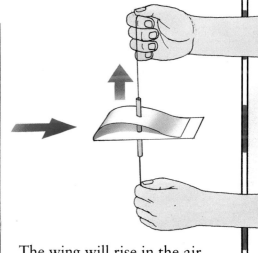

The wing will rise in the air. What does your friend think will happen if he or she blows from the other side?

CATAMARAN

Catamarans have two narrow hulls running along their length that are joined by the main part of the ship. This design spreads the weight of the ship over a large area. Because the hulls are narrow, they displace, or push aside, less water than an ordinary ship with the same capacity. This reduces the drag of the water, which means catamarans can travel very quickly. The wave-piercing catamaran on the right has a maximum speed of 42 knots and a cruising speed of 35 knots. It is 243 feet (74 m) long — just a little longer than a jumbo jet — and 85 feet (26 m) wide. Its engines are linked directly to water jets that propel the catamaran. Other water jets control steering and reversing. Because of the way they spread their weight, catamarans are very stable, and they can be built much larger than hydrofoils. They can carry up to 80 cars as well as passengers. Huge new catamarans, the size of a soccer field, are now being designed that will be able to carry trucks, too (below).

Catamarans, like the one below, provide ferry services in Great Britain, Scandinavia, Australia, and South America.

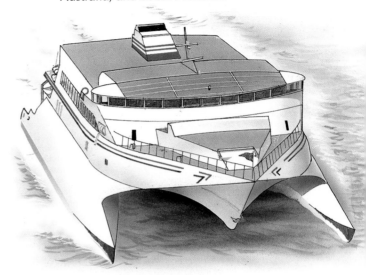

In June 1990, a catamaran called the *Hoverspeed Great Britain* won the Hales Blue Riband Trophy for the fastest crossing of the Atlantic Ocean. It took three days, seven hours, and 54 minutes at an average speed of 36.6 knots.

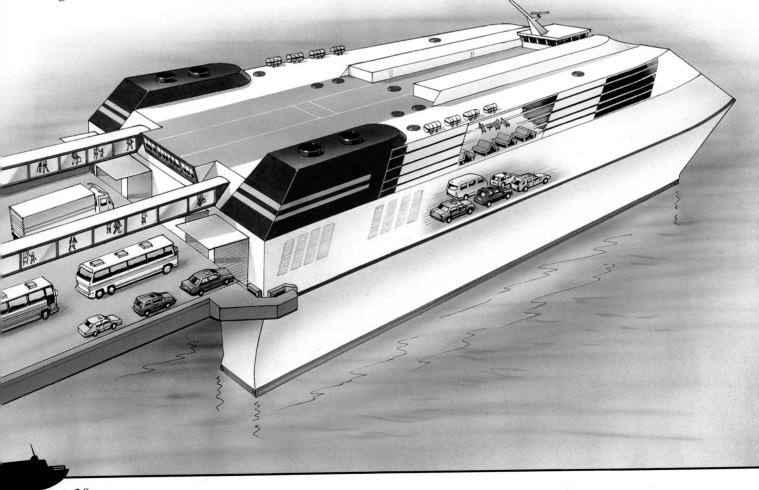

THE FIRST HOVERCRAFT

The first successful hover-craft was designed by Christopher Cockerell in 1959. He figured out how to produce a cushion of air to make the craft fly above the water. The hovercraft's skirt was invented by C.H. Latimer-Needham.

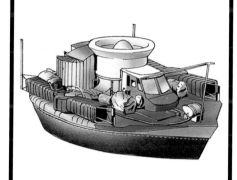

A CUSHION OF AIR

Hovercraft fly about 10 feet (3 m) above the water. Powerful gas turbine engines turn enormous fans that push air downward underneath the craft. The pressure of this air is slightly higher than the surrounding air, so the hovercraft lifts up. The skirt around the craft traps the air and keeps the pressure under the hovercraft higher than it is outside. The skirt is flexible and acts like a shock absorber so that the craft can move smoothly. The engines also turn propellers, which push the hovercraft forward and steer it. Hovercraft can travel at speeds of up to 70 knots. They are large enough to carry cars, which must be arranged carefully on the car deck to distribute their weight evenly.

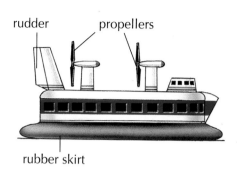

hovercraft at rest

rudder   propellers

rubber skirt

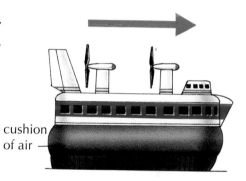

hovercraft in motion

cushion of air

MAKE A HOVERCRAFT

You can make a hovercraft with a food tray and an empty yogurt container. Draw around the base of the yogurt container to mark a circle at the center of the food tray. Cut this out. Cut the base off the yogurt container, and slide it into the hole in the food tray. Using a blow-dryer, blow air through the yogurt pot. The friction between tray and tabletop is reduced by the pressure of the air forced under the tray, so it lifts up and "floats."

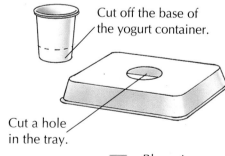

Cut off the base of the yogurt container.

Cut a hole in the tray.

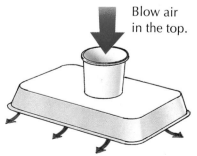

Blow air in the top.

The tray lifts on a cushion of air.

Make two holes through the skirt at one end of the hovercraft. Air escaping through the holes will push the craft in the opposite direction.

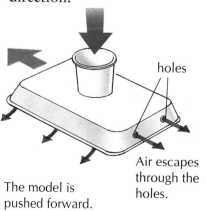

holes

Air escapes through the holes.

The model is pushed forward.

BOATS FOR SPORTS AND RECREATION

Ever since people first figured out how to travel on water, they have wanted to go faster and farther than others. For centuries, there have been races in ships and boats powered by oars or the wind. Nowadays, people have more leisure time and money, so they can enjoy water sports. This has led to many new kinds of sports being developed both for competition and for fun. New materials, designs, types of propulsion, and fuels have led to a wide variety of boats for sports and recreation.

ROWING AND PADDLING

Rowing, canoeing, and kayaking are very popular sports. In rowing, a new oar shape was introduced in 1992, called a cleaver. The blade has a larger surface area than the traditional design, so it moves more water, but it is shorter, so it has less leverage on the water (see page 13). In kayak racing, a newly designed paddle with a curved edge can increase the competitor's speed, saving three seconds every 3,280 feet (1,000 m).

MOTORBOATS

Racing motorboats are designed to compete at high speeds. Some have jet engines, like those used in jet airplanes — others use powerful gasoline or diesel engines. The hulls are designed so that, as the boats speed up, they skim over the waves, reducing the drag of the water so they can go even faster. Jet Skis® also use powerful engines to suck water through a device called an impeller. This forces water at high speed through a nozzle at the back of the ski to push it along.

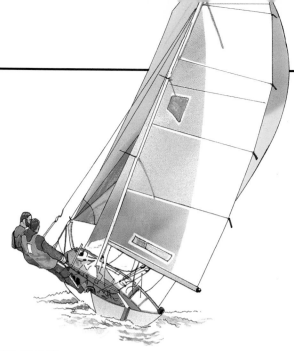

SAILING

To go as fast as possible, sailors want to avoid two problems that reduce their speed. The first is being pushed sideways by the wind. A centerboard or a keel helps to prevent this. The second problem is being pushed too far over by the wind on the sail. Lightweight masts and sails made of new carbon fiber materials make the top of a boat lighter, so it is easier for the centerboard or keel to counterbalance the wind.

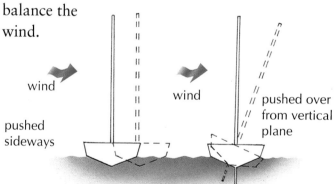

wind

pushed sideways

wind

pushed over from vertical plane

WINGED KEEL

Some large racing yachts now have winged keels. This means the weight of the keel is lower in the

water. The lower the weight, the better the keel counterbalances the force of the wind on the sails. This keeps the yacht more upright, and means the sails can catch more of the wind.

TRIMARANS AND CATAMARANS

Trimarans (with three hulls) and catamarans (with two hulls) make very fast racing yachts. This is because there is less water drag on their long, narrow hulls than with ordinary yachts. They are also very stable and don't lean or heel over too much, which helps them go faster. Lots of motorboats now use a catamaran design, too.

SAILBOARDING

Sailboards are made of fiberglass and nylon, which are cheap enough for lots of people to afford, so sailboarding is very popular. Sailboards also have the advantage of being portable, simple to put together, and easy to sail — after a lot of practice! Sailboards come in all shapes and sizes. Some are designed for speed and others for tricks and jumps.

SHIPS OF THE FUTURE

The designs of ships change either because people need the ship to do new or different things, or because new inventions have produced a technological advance. People in the future will come up with new designs for hulls, new materials to build with, new sources of power, and better engines that won't damage the environment.

SPECIAL NEEDS

Smuggling and piracy are a big problem. In the future, police forces might use ships like this one (above) to stop crime at sea. This ship cannot be detected easily, because it has a specially designed shape that reduces radar echoes, and it uses a remarkable material that absorbs radar pulses. It can locate other ships at night, while staying hidden itself, by using infrared heat sensors or information sent to it by satellite. It also uses sonar to listen to the noises made by other ships or submarines. It can travel at speeds of 45 knots, even in rough seas and can chase, stop, or destroy other ships with its guns, missiles, or directed energy weapons (high-powered lasers).

FUEL ECONOMY

Today, a cargo ship produces the same amount of exhaust fumes as 10,000 cars. New technology is now developing that uses sails shaped like aircraft wings turned on end. The force that lifts an aircraft off the ground can be used to push the ship along. Computers set the sails at the best angle to the wind. This way, ships will be able to save fuel and protect the environment.

POWER AND PROPULSION

As fuels like coal and oil become scarce, and pollution increases, people will develop new ways of powering ships. In the future, they might use magnetohydrodynamic systems that use strong magnetic fields to force seawater through tubes that act like water jets. Or they might use energy from the sun to split water into hydrogen and oxygen. The hydrogen is then burned in special engines, and the only exhaust is water.

MATERIALS

Catamarans (see page 38) and trimarans are well designed, because they spread the weight of a large ship over two or three slim hulls. In the future, ultrastrong and ultralight materials might be developed that will make it possible to build enormous liner-type multi-hulled ships that can carry passengers across the Atlantic Ocean.

GLOSSARY

AIR RESISTANCE The drag of air on objects moving through it.

BOAT Small, open craft usually without any deck.

BOW The front end of a ship or boat.

BUOYANCY The ability of a ship to stay afloat.

CARVEL PLANKING When the external planks of a hull are edge to edge with each other.

CAULKING A method of filling gaps between a ship's planking. Oakum and melted pitch are used to make the hull watertight.

CENTERBOARD A board in the bottom of a dinghy that acts as a keel. The board can be raised and lowered.

CENTERLINE An imaginary line running down the middle of the ship from the bow to the stern.

CLINKER PLANKING When the external planks of a hull overlap the ones below.

DISPLACED WATER Water that is pushed out of the way by an object that is put in it, such as a ship. If the weight of the water pushed aside is heavier than the object, then the object will float.

GYROSCOPIC COMPASS A compass that uses a gyroscope. A gyroscope is a device that always spins on the same axis, and this axis can be set to point to true north. A gyroscopic compass is more accurate than a magnetic compass, because it is not affected by the Earth's magnetic field or any magnetism produced by the metal hull of the ship.

HULL The outer body of a ship or boat.

HYDRODYNAMICS The effects and forces produced by and on water when objects are moving through it.

HYDROPLANE A fin on a submarine that tilts up or down. This makes the submarine move up or down when traveling underwater.

KNOTS The way of measuring speed in water — 1 knot equals 1.15 miles (1.85 km) per hour.

LATITUDE A way of finding out how far north or south of the Equator you are. The Equator is 0° latitude. Other lines of latitude run parallel to the Equator up to 90° at the North and South poles. By calculating your longitude and latitude, you can pinpoint your exact position anywhere on Earth.

LONGITUDE A way of finding out how far east or west of the Prime Meridian you are. Lines of longitude divide the Earth like the segments of an orange — they are farther apart at the Equator and meet at the Poles. By working out your longitude and latitude, you can pinpoint your exact position anywhere on Earth.

MAGNETIC NORTH The Earth's core contains a huge amount of metal that creates an enormous magnetic field over the planet. One end of this magnetic field is very close to but not exactly the same as true north. Magnetic compasses point to the northernmost part of this magnetic field and not to true north. Navigators have to consider this when they are calculating their position using a magnetic compass.

MULTI-HULLED SHIPS Ships, like catamarans or trimarans, that have more than one hull. The hulls are narrower than normal ships, so there is less water drag on multi-hulled craft.

OAKUM Fibers from untwisted ropes. This material was forced into the gaps between planks in ships' hulls and sealed with pitch to make the hulls watertight.

PITCH A sticky, black substance made from tar or wood. It is liquid when hot and hardens when cold, and it is waterproof.

PLIMSOLL LINE A line painted on the outside of a ship's hull that marks where the water level should be when the ship is loaded with cargo in certain conditions or areas.

PRIME MERIDIAN The line of longitude that passes through the Royal Observatory in Greenwich, London. It is 0° longitude.

RADAR An instrument that uses radio waves to measure the distance to an object and its speed and direction.

REEFING Reducing the size of a sail. This is done in strong winds to prevent the ship from being blown over.

RUDDER A flat plate that is hinged to the stern of a ship and used to steer the ship.

SEAWORTHINESS In good condition to be at sea. Ships have to be stable and buoyant to be seaworthy.

SHIP Generally an oceangoing vessel with a deck.

SONAR A device that detects the location and what an object is underwater by using sound waves.

STABILITY A stable ship is able to stay right side up, even in rough waters.

STEAM TURBINE An engine in which steam generated in a separate boiler is used to drive a set of blades called a turbine. The turbine rotates thousands of times per minute, and a gearbox then transfers this power directly to the propeller.

STERN The back part of a ship or boat.

TRUE NORTH The northernmost part of the Earth, also known as the North Pole. The lines of latitude and longitude north of the Equator meet here. This is one end of the Earth's axis, and the South Pole is at the other end. The Earth spins on this north-south axis.

U-BOAT German submarine of World Wars I and II. *U-boat* is short for *Unterseeboot* or "undersea boat."

INDEX

A
air resistance, 10, 44
Atlantic Ocean, 38, 43

B
biremes, 13
Blue Riband Trophy, 38
bow, 16, 44
Brunel, Isambard Kingdom, 28
buoyancy, 23, 44
Bushnell, David, 34

C
canoes, 10–11, 40
cargo ships, 14, 16, 22–23, 43
Cartesian divers, 33
carvel planking, 20
catamarans, 38, 41, 43
caulking, 16, 44
centerboards, 41, 44
Charlotte Dundas, 28
China, 14, 15, 18, 26
chronometers, 24, 25, 26
clinker planking, 16, 20, 44
Cockerell, Christopher, 39
coffin ships, 22
compasses, 26–27
container ships, 22
Cook, Captain, 24, 25
coracles, 10
cross staffs, 27

D
David submarines, 34
diesel engines, 31, 33, 34, 35, 40
displaced water, 22, 38, 44
drag, 38, 44
dugout canoes, 11

E
Egypt, 8, 14, 18
Elise, 30
engines, 28–31, 33, 34–35, 39, 40, 42, 43

F
ferries, 31, 38
Forlanini, Enrico, 36

G
galleys, 12–15
gasoline engines, 31, 34, 35, 40
gas turbine engines, 31, 39
Genghis Khan, 10
Great Eastern, 28
Greece, 12, 13
Greenwich Meridian, 26, 44

gyroscopic compasses, 26, 44

H
Harrison, John, 25, 26
Heyerdahl, Thor, 8
hovercraft, 36, 39
Hoverspeed Great Britain, 38
hulls, 10, 14, 16, 20, 32, 34, 36, 38, 40, 41, 42, 43, 44
hydrofoils, 31, 36–37, 38
hydroplanes, 33, 44

J
Jet Skis®, 40
junks, 18

K
kayaks, 10, 40
keels, 18, 19, 41
Kendall, Larcum, 25
Kon Tiki, 8

L
Latimer-Needham, C.H., 39
latitude, 24, 26, 27, 44
lifeboats, 23
lighthouses, 24
liners, 30, 43
lodestone, 26
longitude, 24, 25, 26, 27, 44
Lusitania, 30

M
magnetic compasses, 26, 27, 44
magnetohydrodynamic systems, 43
Mary Rose, 20
masts, 16, 41
Mauretania, 30
Mayer, Johann, 27
merchant ships, 14, 16, 22–23, 43
Mir submersibles, 34
Mongols, 10
motorboats 40, 41

N
navigation, 24–27
nuclear power, 31, 34, 35

O
oars, 12, 13, 14, 18, 40
outriggers, 11

P
Pacific Ocean, 8, 11
paddle wheels, 28, 29, 31
paddling, 10, 12, 13, 14, 40
papyrus boats, 8

periscopes, 32
piston engines, 31
Plimsoll marks, 22, 44
Prime Meridian, 26, 44
propellers, 29, 30, 31, 36, 39
punting, 14

R
radar, 27, 32, 42, 44
rafts, 8–9
reed boats, 9
reefing, 18, 44
Roman Empire, 12, 14
rowing, 12–14, 18, 40
rudders, 12, 14, 15, 33, 44

S
sailboards, 41
sails, 8, 11, 14, 16–18, 41, 43
seaworthiness, 22, 44
sextants, 24, 27
sonar, 32, 42, 44
stability, 11, 16, 19, 20, 22, 23, 38, 44
steamships, 28–31, 44
steering, 12, 14
submarines, 31, 32–35, 42, 44
submersibles, 34
supertankers, 28

T
tacking, 19
tillers, 15
Titanic, 32, 34
Titicaca, Lake, 9
Trajan's Column, 12
trimarans, 41, 43, 44
triremes, 13
turbine engines, 30, 31, 35, 39, 44
Turtle, 34

U
U-boats, 32, 44

V
Vikings, 16–19

W
Wales, 10
warships, 16, 20–23, 31, 32
wheels, steering, 15
whipstaffs, 15
winds, 11, 17–19, 40, 43

Y
yachts, 19, 41